MW01004924

Frances
of the Wider Field

~~Laura Van Prooyen~~

Laura Van Prooyen

To Heidi —
My friend in poetry.
♡ Laura
9/2021

LILY POETRY REVIEW BOOKS

Copyright © 2021 by Laura Van Prooyen

Published by Lily Poetry Review Books
223 Winter Street
Whitman, MA 02382

https://lilypoetryreview.blog/

ISBN: 978-1-7347869-6-5

All rights reserved. Published in the United States by Lily Poetry Review
Books.
Library of Congress Control Number: 2020949589

Cover Art: "Grow" by Christine K. Harris

for my mother and her mother

Acknowledgements

I am grateful to the editors of the following journals where these poems first appeared, sometimes in slightly different forms:

Adroit: "Avenue F" and "Your Face Belongs to the Lily"

American Poetry Review: "As Always, Thirty Years Between Us" and "The Calumet Region"

Birmingham Review: "Head of Clover," "Frances of Pleiades," "Rush of Pulse and Song"

Blackbird: "San Antonio Dogs," "Sister"

The Collagist: "Reconstruction" and "You hear the gods of your childhood whispering"

Cortland Review: "Properties of Change," "Joke," "Parting the Dome of Dark Skies," "Lilac Full of Bees" and "Inflammation of the Nerves"

Diode: "Against Nostalgia"

The Greensboro Review: "Is a Temple," and "Hill Country, Unreachable"

Missouri Review online: "Location, Frances"

National Poetry Review: "Going Home"

Pleiades: "Split"

Ploughshares: "Lineage Fragment" and "Frances of the Cadillac"

Poet Lore: "Postcard from Texas"

Poetry Northwest: "The Post-Hole Digger Dismantles My Mother's Psyche"

Prairie Schooner: "Elegy to My Mother's Mind," "I Will Grow Old in My Bed," "My Mother in the Winter Zoo," "My History in Sand and Light," and "Psalm 23 ½"

Rhino: "Imaging Test"

The Southern Review: "My Mother in Pixels" and "Thirteen Ways of Living Next to Jenny"

Spoon River Poetry Review: "Dark Praise," "Flood," "Norther," "My Brother Defines Success," "Chronic," "One of Those Days"

"Elegy to My Mother's Mind," "My Mother in the Winter Zoo," "I Will Grow Old in My Bed," and "Psalm 23 ½" received the Annual Glenna Luschei Prairie Schooner Award.

Thank you, Artist Foundation of San Antonio, for generous support. Thanks to Eileen Cleary for believing in these poems and to everyone at Lily Poetry Review Books. Also, thanks to these poets for helping me shape this book: Sheila Black, Jenny Browne, Joanne Diaz, Ann Hudson, Hoa Nguyen, and Alexandra van de Kamp. Finally, these poems belong to my mom, Patricia Van Prooyen, from whom many stories were withheld, but who made sure my life was rich with understanding and memory—thanks.

Contents

The work of memory collapses time.
—Walter Benjamin

AVENUE F

Looking for you in the street,
I said to the crab apple tree, *You are Frances.*

To asbestos shingles, *What keeps you*
in place? A car with new Firestones

stopped at the light rumbles, *We will never die,*
though your hands could do more work. I remember you

wringing starched sheets between rollers,
hanging them on the line to dry. I've never been

that clean in all my life. God will never reward me
in the way I hope. Frances, you polished

the baby's shoes. You made silver shine.
You pinned prayers to your head and shook

floor mats free of stones. The street can't hold
my desires. Who painted those white lines?

Frances, there's a dog in the road.

Imaging Test

                    my mother's brain

scans the dense fields
                    oh child, you are covered

dirt kicks up behind a wagon
                              and now the girl

will get no pink peppermints

                    the amazing machine
prints lines and numbers

              there is your father
                    in one stroke, a graph

the bulldozer

        clears the land for the highway

here is a tuna casserole
                    here are your children

eating only the crumbled potato chips
                                    off the top

your son now drives big rigs

              your daughter never got off the swings

the amazing machine
                    skips rope

a child tells you your mother is dead

                                 here is a braided rug
here is your cousin

              who died last week

pulling you on a towel
                 across your grandmother's floor

       you will not stop

there, your daughter
                  no longer has cancer

   your grandchild   which one?

                       beats a drum in the band and

soon, your boyfriend

       will be back at the gas station, washing buses

          you'll bring him a sandwich

comb his hair

          this amazing machine

rests on a pillow
                it's cold in there

SPLIT

Mother, I wish I could twin myself and tuck you in
to your blanket cocoon. You say the cold eats at your bones,

and I know, because last time I heard crumbling marrow
roll through you like rain. Mother, there are feathers

stuck in my throat. I wish for a twin with telepathic lips
against your good ear. Let her relay that yesterday

a swarm of cedar waxwings picked clean your daughter's
ligustrum of fruit. The daughter who moved to warmer climes,

because you said—remember?—everything would be okay.
Let this more beautiful child help you find the perfect tilt,

suspend your legs, undo gravity's pressure. I made sure
she knows your fleece throw should fold under your feet,

that your worn pillow is to cradle your head,
and it's your left ear to which she should bend when she says:

your far-away daughter sends love from her new, green yard.
Her voice chimes like mine, but may sound sweeter as it swirls

into your inner ear. Mother, don't let her vibrations fool you
if through thin cochlear fluid you hear:

I am the girl who loves you best. My twin is prone to lie,
even as she leans, her silken hair glancing your eyes. The laws

are different here. From twelve hundred miles away, I duplicate.
I splinter. I fly. Mother, I float to your ceiling, drift over

your body. Your body my heart once beat in,
where as a dark cluster of cells I began furiously to split.

LILACS FULL OF BEES

Didn't I just tell this story?
Didn't Frances just clean her gutters?
Didn't she polish her car?
Take a toothbrush to the white-walled tires?

Didn't Frances say, *Just a minute?*
With what voice?

Didn't she listen to the radio in the dark?
Didn't she have feet?
Didn't she soak them, rub her corned toes?

Who here knows the story?

I remember an organ and hymns
from another time
in another language.

Is a sigh a word? Is a body a word?
Is a tongue the beginning?

I can't undo these questions.

Who remembers the clothesline?
Bleached sheets?
The lilacs full of bees?

Where there's a voice there's an answer.
Didn't Frances say, *Don't forget
my hairbrush, my slippers, my teeth?*

Weren't you there? Weren't you listening?
Didn't she have hands?

Don't you hear me? Isn't this your story?

PSALM 23$^{1/2}$

I left the sloping bank of Thorn Creek, the cracked asphalt
        of 170th street and still windows washed with vinegar shine.

Bricks hosed and cleared of vines hold on
        to mortar, decayed. On a ladder my father scoops leaves

from the gutter never putting off till tomorrow
        what he can do today. How vain

to think distance might change the lines on my palm
        or the chapter and verse lodged under

my tongue. The Lord is my shepherd,
        but I don't want the green pasture or the still water

or a doily under my tea. I don't want
        the doll with eyes that open and close or the shattered oak

with one living limb that my mother insists on saving.
        I don't want to sit under the clothesline,

with my mother comparing our feet,
        noting the veins on our legs look the same. I know

exactly from where I came. From the field,
        from onions stinging the air and my eyes, from

long swaths of land and longer Sundays
        spooled out like rough ribbon braided through my hair.

FRANCES OF THE PLEIADES

The afternoon has grown quiet, Frances. My cat's ear
turns toward the sound of chimes. If I said,

God is in the air, I could as easily have said,
the child's un-creased face is a revelation.

What does this matter to you? You're the jingle
of keys, you're the motorcycle revving a block away.

See, today was full of auspicious signs,
and though you never believed in stars, it's you

rising as my neighbor scuttles home from work.
Is it wrong to say there's something luminous

in my blood? Is it possible that the girl
who buried the gecko covered *you* with stones?

Frances of all things and of no things. Don't
get angry when I sing the wrong words. Don't forget

the peppermints, white as stars, wrapped in tissue.
Memory cannot undo the future. Frances, if I said,

tonight I thank the seven sisters, it's really
the blue dust of God between them. Or you.

INFLAMMATION OF THE NERVES

it's just a case of shingles   latent virus

re-activated   in the body

         what kind of answer

is a shingle? a house

     built on rock, roofed with *don't pay them no mind*

my arm is hot
        fever shudder   search

search for   cause/treatment

     cause for

big rash   *small snake*   *hell's fire*   What kind

     of answer is: "Your father

had shingles. Not too bad. Just covered them up

     till they were gone."

I cover up

     long-sleeved   secret blisters

on the nerve road of my left arm   hidden

     virus   all these years in my cells

how do you define

        silence?   Quiet does not mean

dead   Quiet does not mean   not listening

      activation of the latent virus is poorly understood

no one knows what triggers

      the secret blister   in 92 degrees and sun

treatment   limits travel of nerve bodies

to the endings of the skin   Quiet

      does not mean   *don't pay them no mind*

Hill Country, Unreachable

Out here, I hook messages
to vulture wings. I tell feral hogs

about my sister's cancer,
and they run away. Cliffs

slap back my voice. *God?*
I don't know if silence

is an ocean. I'm swirling
in a canyon riddled with shells.

Hear me, my sister has cancer
and every time they go in,

they find more. A new spot
or score of cells exposed,

like the scorpion you didn't want
to find under the stone.

DARK PRAISE

My sister had to cut off her breasts. My daughter
asks for a new pancreas. I may be a fool
to believe in goodness. What a risk to love
the soldier who tells me he was hauling ass
when a girl ran in front of his tank. He can't
sleep. I can't sleep. I can't shake the sound
he said her body made. My sister
is a whole new you. She changed her hair,
her name, and she looks good. My daughter
could go blind. We don't talk kidneys
or transplants or amputated feet.
The soldier told me blood is unreal
on a windshield. He can't sleep. He likes
to drink. I like to drink, too. I raise a glass
to my sister's new breasts. Praise my daughter's
needles, insulin, blood tests. I drink for the girl
who, if there's mercy, never knew what was coming.

SAN ANTONIO DOGS

Dear Happiness: Tonight a trio of dogs
sat at the crosswalk waiting for the light to change.
Red. I stopped. They trotted across the street, two mottled mutts
and a Chihuahua whose legs spun like wheels to keep up.
Right across San Pedro and down the sidewalk,
their tails up, noses pointed toward purpose. Dear Happiness:
I never cared for dogs, but they're everywhere here.
When I miss my mother, who was once the mother
of all happiness, I see dogs. San Antonio dogs.
The one in Olmos Basin, a scrappy mix of ribs and hunger
hurrying across the road. Or the stray I found panting
in a shred of shade under an agave in whose muddy eyes
spun the tires of the Buick Le Sabre from the summer vacation
when my mother nearly drove us into the lake. Dear Happiness:
What laughter when flecked with mud! Or so it once was,
when laughter was easy. More often now, I drive Frio Avenue
to work. Not that there's not happiness in high tension
wires, in bouncing over the tracks by the building
with *Monterrey Lounge* faded on bricks, where knotted curtains
in wide-open windows swing. Where, on the roof
of the garage, a bullish dog rushes out to the rusted edge
barking down onto the street. He runs so fast, I fear
he's not going to stop. One day when that dog wasn't there
I circled the block, waited at the curb,
but vacancy jabbed sharper than his barks. How thin
the air felt without him guarding the roofline, without his body,
dirty white, like tissues my mother used to tuck into her Sunday purse.

LOCATION: FRANCES

When I say Frances, I mean the maple trunk
bulging through chain-link. I mean the pit bull
with spiked collar who lives on the other side.

I say Frances and I sound like a leaking bike tire.
Frances: my purple Schwinn, my flowered banana-seat.
My legs pumping through the subdivision

that springs from the field. Frances
rides on the air. You might say, *I don't understand,*
and I'd say, *This is not my voice.* It's something

in the leaves that keeps speaking. Something that saw
me as a child, rubbed a coin on the sole of my foot.
When I say Frances, I mean a woman. I mean

a place. The dead cling to the land. The living cling
to a story that, like currency, changes hands.

LINEAGE FRAGMENT

before words   pulsing your mother   calling you
naming you you don't know who named   her voice
        unrecorded   between fibers   cells
of your skin that never slough off   her blood
      on the delivery room floor   she held you you heard
before she left her body you left her body
        with force with force enough to

                              she loved you you heard
heard   the hole your head left   with a rush
    of blood   that would not stop   she would not stop
      reaching for you   heard   from whispers   pity
voices   thin as Bible paper   whisper threads   braided
    what they said what they didn't   pity
heard   your own skate blades   scraping   her
    favorite frozen pond   you heard   nothing

from your father   who dressed you   in fine wool
photographed his grief
                    cheeks touched with a bit of color   your
father   never got over your face   her face in your face   her
    shape always near   your skin   never
sloughed off   the touch of the mother you never
        knew   your face   rubbed clean   by the mother

you came to know   woman of metallic grief   took up
        the baby   held up   your father   darned his socks
filled absence   with figs   mother
        who starched her mouth shut who saw in your mouth

her dead sister   dust and stars   the mother
     of lilies   buckled shoes   tightly-braided hair
          who reached into loss and pulled out a rake   cleared
the ground of pebbles   burned debris   swept
clean   your slate
          her slate   her sister's slate that wouldn't be swept at all

WINTER HAIBUN

Rain softens San Antonio, like a Chicago spring where after
a punishing spell a crocus might poke through mud next to a
melting pile of snow in a debris-pocked yard. Change is subtle
here. Like a soft lens, edges blur to ease the harsh line between
what was, what is, and what you hoped for. Seasons slur, one
long word you can't put your finger on.

against the fog
a bright orange on a neighbor's tree
tells me where I am not

ONE OF THOSE DAYS

—after Barbara Ras

You can't have it all, but you can have old asbestos shingles
painted a brand new blue. You can have
the black crooked-jaw cat that sleeps on your legs,
follows you to the kitchen, curls beside you on your chair.
You can have the hand of a 10-year-old on your knee,
lifting one finger at a time for you to paint silver
on each little nail. You can travel to a new city,
alert and alive as you walk on unknown streets,
you can sit beside the ocean, but you can't change
sorrow. You can have love, even when it's like apple cider
vinegar, that sour cure for so many ills. You can take
your father out for a fresh peach sundae, his dentures
clacking as he tells you the exact etch and cut
he wants on his own grave stone. You can have cattails
in the ditch, the long bus ride where you're the first one
on, the last one off, and you know every child at every stop.
You can move closer to joy, your yard flowering
with *bougainvillea* and *esperanza* and still regret
touching hairless baby gerbils when their mother
killed and buried in wood shavings her whole brood.
You can have manure in the spring and call it sweet. You can't
count on faith to stroke your cheek, but if your mother
hauls a pair of roller skates down from the attic, the ancient ones
with a key, you can unlock them and slide them to your size.
In a pile of junk, you can still find boots that fit. And when you sort
through childhoods stiff with mold, your acceptance
quietly throws clothes into garbage bags, drives them
to a dumpster, gives up what won't be missed. You
won't know in what ways you failed, hundreds of possibilities
thread your sheets. You can't have it all, but you can

still count on the evergreen. You can summon the sound
of your dad's electric clippers, of your mother's metal rake.
Your fingers scrape through dirt like tines.
You gather cuttings, the sun warm on your back.

FRANCES OF THE CADILLAC

Under her tongue, there was a story.
In her mouth, nails. Frances hammered license plates
to the back wall of her garage. There

hang the years that sunk like a foot in loose soil.
That rusted like a hinge. Whose hand or what machine
etched the numbers that cruised along

in the exhaust of a town that no longer exists?
This is what happens when I check my wristwatch.

Frances drives her leather-topped Cadillac
between the electrical signals of my brain. There's
a railroad crossing, and I don't understand

the way she's looking at me. Her body tells me something
happened. Her arms so thin, veins show
when she rolls up her sleeves. Still, if I were drowning

I know Frances would save me. She might throw
a string of black pearls. She might offer a broom handle,
worn from her sweeping. She'd pull me to the edge,

push pennies from my lungs. But, it's the bells
of the crossing that make it hard to breathe.

ELEGY FOR MY MOTHER'S MIND

We're walking inside your mind where it's beginning to snow,
and no matter how quickly I shovel, the path will go blank.

Where you'll lose the child who picked every last tulip
you waited a solid Chicago winter to watch bloom. Lose the girl

who pedaled her Schwinn up and back the driveway while you
fried bacon behind the evergreens in an electric pan so the house

wouldn't smell. But this night, grackles above us blacken the tree
and you hold on to me as you get into the car. Together, we go

to the store where you try on every clearance-marked blouse
and buy nothing. You're forgetting sadness, too. That pool

where you used to swim with an armload of bricks,
where no slow tug of a rope could pull you from the bottom.

You're forgetting about anyone but you, when before dawn
on the piano you pound *Great Balls of Fire* and *The Old Rugged Cross*

and whistle in searing vibrato. You gift Dollar Store Kleenex
pour beans into wine bottles, lift my chin and say, *I'm so glad*

you were born—then your pupils widen and tunnel back to before
I was here, before my brothers or sister, before you lost your father,

a time of buses and rain, of radio static, and for a minute
you're far from me, so I reach for your trembling hand.

THE CORNER OF YES AND YESTERDAY

Tell me about the station, the candy rack,
the door. Was there a shopkeeper bell?

Who was the boy washing buses? Who
counted the change? Money has no place in dreams.

Or in mouths, but I suck on coins to take back
the elements of the earth. And you,

why do you pull a long blade of grass
and place it between your lips? Why pick the dandelion,

rubbing yellow on your wrist? One sure weed,
one swipe of color. One tough root.

Those were the days. These are the nights.
Feel the tin-twinged air?

There's the boy pumping gas. A girl
sliding her foot along the wheel.

What do you make of the flickering lights?
Is this place about to close?

My History in Sand and Light

My mother was having one of her days. She lay on the blanket in the sun
too long. Her egg salad sandwich beside her spoiled. I know this,
because it's the story she told. Sand filtered under the floor mats

when she drove. Sand stuck to her calves. Inescapable,
for days in her hair and clothes. I was not there. I was light

if I was anything at all. The air, unobstructed by my height.
Gnats swarmed the forsythia. She swore they'd burn
from the yellow. It hurt her eyes. In the house,

she asked questions of the dark. She poked the window shade
with a nail. Her future was listening, so she spoke again.

The Post-Hole Digger Dismantles My Mother's Psyche

It wasn't about the forsythia,
      but that her father had planted it. It wasn't

that her father planted it, but that he died. He died,
and she found out coming up the stairs at Ben Franklin

      where she had just purchased curtains. Curtains

that were delivered the day after the funeral, that were hung
in the breezeway. That hang in the breezeway, still, that room

      that's hardly a room, but windows, walls of windows

that when cranked open, unhinge the boundary between within
and without, between her father and flowering limbs.

HEAD OF CLOVER

Inside my mother's head of clover
we find a wider field. Thicker, ruddy air and a girl

standing by the road. She is the one who lost
her mother. The one who as a baby
had her face scrubbed, a gold bracelet fitted

around her fat little wrist. What a clean,
motherless baby with patent leather shoes.
The girl's legs are long now. And in the open,

a speck on a wide horizon, she rolls the cuffs
of her jeans. She pulls out her bike. Plowed rows
haven't yet been planted. Crows haven't yet come

to pick the seeds. Does the girl ride? Does she cross
the creek, head to town? Clover, so much clover,
pushes out dull white blooms. It must be

afternoon. The girl ties the tails of her checked blouse
into a knot at her waist. Either way, the road is long.

YOU HEAR THE GODS
OF YOUR CHILDHOOD WHISPERING

everywhere. Under a lifted rock, the pill bug says *yes,*
turn a little to better see. Or they rustle in the maple
behind the chicken coop, stir in the feed.
Sometimes they hide in thick frost on a window
where you press a penny against the pane.
They tell you it's okay to be cold. They tell you
you haven't missed as much as you think.
They pinprick your eyelids as you try to fall asleep,
retracing your school bus route: Sonny's house,
his yellow dog chained to a circle of dirt. Then,
some days, the gods go silent. You wait, and walk
the cracked stretch of your street. Wait and wait,
but the mite on the wing of the goldfinch
never sounds. You know the gods are here, muffled
in your sweater's red threads. They gather
in loose strands of hair you tuck behind your ear.
You wait on your paint-peeled stairs. A cricket
in the grass goes on a long time. Listen, listen.

MY FACE BELONGS TO THE LILY

Whatever stones I'd turn over, Frances made me
put them back. When I'd unravel the hose,

I never could restore the stack of coils. If I laughed,
I'd see her study my open mouth. Sometimes,

I'd stay quiet beside her,
                     fingers working leaf or vine or soil.

There's nothing that grows greater than silence.

She never said, *Listen.* Never said, *This dirt
lines your lungs.* I breathed and breathed and the sleeves

of her work-blouse wore thin. I didn't know

       where my knuckles sprung from
               or the freckled legacy of my arm.

MY MOTHER IN PIXELS

I see you on Skype. My face
on the lower right corner of the screen.

Dad stands behind you, says
together you've cleared the den of magazines.
At the same time, we weakly smile.

My whole life I've been told how much I look like you,
but I've never seen our faces together in motion.

We tighten our lips when Dad says
Uncle Ray is filling with fluid again.
When silent, we squint.

Your blind eye is looking good, and I tell you.
We push up our lids and laugh. Your eyes,

so often lost in those sockets, regain their spark.

POSTCARD FROM TEXAS

This morning, miss you means the hawthorn's
blooming, air so sweet it threatens to attract bees.
Miss you is a street full of pecans that roll under
my feet. I falter, yes. Miss you means not falling,
means this distance feels bigger than Texas, than
long tall clouds high enough to be laced with snow.

LINEAGE FRAGMENT

She taught the girl how to roll dough thin, but Frances
didn't teach me. I was too wild

to crimp a crust. Once, in a fit, I took off my shoe,
raised it above my head, but never meant to throw it.

A stranger at the post office recognized someone's face
in my face, noted I must be near

to Frances. Said I must be part of the bouquet. I didn't know
any bloom beyond lilacs, except for violets

scattered in the grass. I couldn't see then
where my face belonged. I didn't know my cheekbone

was 100 years old, or that my mouth
wasn't mine, or my eyes creased in laughter had gone before.

ONCE, A FIELD

Wrapped in her red sweater, Frances walked
against the wind. First when fields were open

and onions stung the air. Then when bare beams
rose into frames, reaching up through fertile soil.

Split-levels took shape and filled with strangers.
Frances walked among them, where there used to be

no boundaries, where before lives stacked up
in this place, the horizon shone unobscured.

FOURTH GRADE AUTOBIOGRAPHY

—after Donika Kelly

We have subdivisions where there used to be
fields, so there are houses and I have friends.
My favorite thing is Bosco on ice cream. More
Bosco than ice cream, and my brother's
make fun of me for that. Call me fat. Laugh
when I cry. Mom says they tease me
because they love me. I'm afraid
of the living room when the lights are off.
I believe in the noises I hear in the basement.
I only got the paddle once from my dad,
because I couldn't help it. I was so scared
I peed. My grandma lives next door
and sees everything. She bakes cookies
every Saturday. My favorite is *Jan Hagel*
and the one with potato chips crumbled in.
She makes me tea, and I dip in saltines
till they're like a limp sheet. We have
lily of the valleys under the maple between
our houses. My bedroom faces the tree. Faces
my grandma's and Thorn Creek Church
where Donna and I ring the bell and run. Donna
cut her bangs and blamed it on me. She's Polish
and Catholic, and people from Holy Ghost
play bingo and drink beer. My dad drinks
in Wisconsin. We go to Eagle River.
It's my favorite thing in the whole world.
I know that the lake is better than a whole summer
of going to the pool. I get to stay up late. One year
there was a girl in the cottage next door.

She used nail clippers to cut the letter K
into her heel. She didn't think I saw. By the fire,
my dad puts his arm around my mom.
My brothers throw frogs into the flames. I hate that,
but I love that my hair fills with smoke,
and I can even smell it on my pillow the next day.

FLOOD

When the city was submerged, all was quiet,
except for bullfrogs spilled onto the road,
their throaty chorus, a song of displacement,

now muted by acres of muddied trees and Olmos Basin
filled with trash. The water has gone, leaving me thirsty
in a South Texas afternoon at a stoplight, eating exhaust

as heat rises in waves. This spot, under 10-feet last week,
was murky as the algae-laced Wisconsin lake
where every June my family unfurled. I don't remember

thirst. I remember ping-pong, bloodsuckers, late-night fires.
Mom frying fish. Running barefoot. Ticks. The bubble
of the Buick's rear window, the small cabin

swallowed by trees. My whole childhood could fit on the tip
of a lit cigarette. Or could be carved on a turtle's shell
to sink and emerge for the next forty years.

JOKE

Smoke bomb   thrown in

the fish house
        my brother   gasping   hands

around his neck

choking
           choke choking I jumped

on my Uncle Billy's back
pummeled his back

      open
           the door

open open
                my brother!

      behind the fish house

by the guts
          laughing

my brother
        cough-laugh-coughing

Uncle Billy beer-slurred
              sunburnt

                    laughing

but I was not

GATHERING

The kitchen table was but a plank
to me. When empty, it was dark as Dam Lake,

where Uncle Billy threw Phillip to shake his fear
of water. Weeknight dinners, my brothers

spit-whispered insults until I would cry and leave.
On Sundays, the table was covered in cloth,

dressed with our best and roast. I'd pull up my chair,
but around my legs, I'd swear there were leeches.

SUNDAY (ROAST)

It's a gravy-stained apron, a can of peas. It's summer! Snap
fresh beans. It's winter. Roast is roast is roast is a holiday turkey
a deviant turkey is lighter gravy is put out the flowered china, please. Leave
the cracklings in the pan. Add starch. Slow stir. Roast done right falls apart.
Snivelcheese is small shreds of (in this case) meat, the best and tastiest
that never make it, never make it to the table. Roast forever roast
mashed potato forever followed on a good day with sweet treats. Followed
with a toothpick. Roast forever the platter forever roast the fat slick.

QUESTIONS FOR FRANCES

If I touch the bruise on your arm, is that memory?
Why do you call me your flower?
When I rang the church bell, did I hear your voice?
Why aren't you answering my questions?
Why don't I remember you laughing?
Is that you laughing?
Is it?
Do you understand that we're going in circles?
That time is mashed like potatoes?
Is your apron gravy-stained?
Do you really believe idle hands are the devil's workshop?
That we're all going in that hand basket to hell?
Why don't I remember the words to your songs?
Why don't you sing me a hymn?
Make the leaves your chorus?
And the wind a big fat melody?
What should I say if I'm questioned?
That trees make excellent music?
That you never used your voice to sing?
That once upon a time there was a town?
A crabapple tree?
A swing?
That faith can be called corn, coffee, and kitchen soap?

THE CALUMET REGION

Truth at my brother's oil change shop is few customers.
Beauty is the woman who drives her car over the pit, accidentally

steps on the gas instead of the brake, pinning a man to her hood,
shattering his back through the window. Beauty can be broken,

can be a crumbling hospital like St. James where I was born
in the hallway because the doctor was too slow. Of that story

my mother can laugh, but birthing my brother, she was knocked out
against her will with gas. She woke to find bruises all over

her baby's head. Truth means that the doctor's names
are not part of the story. That after years of telling and retelling,

my mother sees what she can bear. A small, hurt thing that needs her.
Like the town she'll never leave where people talk with a harsh,

nasal southside "a" and say *melk* instead of *milk*. Where beauty
has something to do with highway noise, with grass breaking

through the cracks, with the kicked-in door on the foreclosed home,
where someone left the windows open and let the house fill with rain.

My Brother Defines Success

Out on the boat, a cold Leinenkugal is all the fish he needs.
Slack line. Slack jaw. Still water and a swarm of gnats. If
the Ozinga job comes through, he'll be in a cement truck
14 hours a day. Come through, fish. Come through, another
year. Sidewalks need to be poured, true enough. Slack sun,
going down and he needs a sweatshirt now. He needs another
beer, a waterbug to look at, a fish to get away. He was born
for this lake. For listening with his good ear.

TUESDAY

Angel fixes my leaking roof, and I say, *Thank you—*
where are your wings? I listen tirelessly

to the rain. Frances, if that thrumming is you,
I'm not satisfied. What do I expect to hear?

Angel's a man with grackle-black hair
and a missing front tooth. I shake his hand,

wash the knives, bake a potato.
In the next room, my girl's conversation

with her cat opens my head like an umbrella.
The clouds could fall all night, and I'd sit here

waiting for a book to levitate. For the Post-it
to prove I exist. Give me 10 minutes,

and let me forget my desires. Forget
the questions in my swollen mouth.

ELEGY WITH CATS IN IT

Every summer there was a new cat.
That was before my father let animals indoors. Before

the subdivision. Jenny moved behind us, played tennis
against our garage door, and my mother spread quilts

on the lawn. Before I knew bowling night meant my Dad
with too many beers, my uncle driving his squad car

through a wall. In the Salty and Pepper days, I'd bike
to Wright's Barnyard for skee-ball and mini-golf, walk

on Wednesdays to Lan-Oak Lanes, hang with my mom
and the smoky ladies of weekly leagues. Before

she needed one arm to prop the elbow of the other
just to lift a gallon of milk. We buried the remains of summer

cats in the horse-shoe garden. Then the garden became
a strip, now it's a stamp where my mother sticks fake flowers

in sight of her spot in the den. She tells me she's happy
in her square of sun. Cozy, like Mama who gave birth

in a box in the basement, who curled her body
in warm air by the foot of the fridge—the longest-lived cat,

even longer than her runt we kept, because we couldn't take
Mama's meowing when we gave her babies away.

THIRTEEN WAYS OF LIVING
NEXT TO JENNY

I
Do not look into the eye
of Jenny.

II
Squirt the whole bottle
of Amway soap
into the sand box, and deny it
when confronted by Jenny.

III
Do not see Jenny
sitting on your picnic table
watching your television
through your window.

IV
Know your god
is not Jenny's God.

V
You cannot change
that the road is a graveyard
for Jenny's cats.

VI
When Jenny is out of sight
there is no Jenny.

VII
With your friends,
crank call Jenny. If you tell her
you want an abortion,
she'll pray with you until she gives up
and puts the phone next to
Christian radio.

VIII
After dark, feed the skinny dog
of Jenny.

IX
When the grass is freshly cut
and you lounge under the maple
and eat a strawberry right off the plant
you know the earth belongs
neither to you, nor Jenny.

X
Jenny is one. You are one.
You will not be one
with Jenny.

XI
Once there was a field,
there were onions, and a woman
who farmed them, until she got too old
and her children without her blessing
sold her home, and then
there was Jenny.

XII
The church bell is ringing.
Jenny must be praying.

XIII
The tire swing is sturdy.
The rut in the ground is deep.
Flying in yellow light,
once I mistook my shadow
for Jenny's.

Is a Temple

Why did Jenny and I come down
for Sunday breakfast in nothing but cotton
underwear, in new bras and bodies,
to eat coffee cake and hard-boiled eggs?

This is the way it was. Her dad smiled, switched
the radio to classical music. Jenny's mom,
in her lumpy robe, stared off into space.
Her older brother busied his eyes
with a cereal box, the comics. Jenny
and I, both in panties, cracked and peeled jagged shells.

At home, I never left my room without clothes.
At Jenny's I'd sit with my thighs sticking
to the chair. With back and shoulders straight,
so my stomach wouldn't roll. I didn't know

just yet (or did I hope) that my body
could be something to want
to touch, especially the hour before church.

AT THE ROLLER RINK

Frances, you shine like a glow stick strung
from my neck. Hum through orange wheels,

rounding the track. The disco ball drops
and it's so *gezzelig*, swirling lights cozy-up the room.

I'm going backwards. A century of muscle
grips my bones. I was slow to embrace

my too-long limbs, but didn't breeze
forever away. Even if I skate fast as I can,

looking over my shoulder at every turn.

Sister

When we shared the same bed, I'd wake to your absence.
I'd watch you at the dresser before dawn

brushing your hair. You never hid from me:
your mole, your white breasts. The day you left home,

I rode my bike hard and way past dark. Without you
I feared pennies pressed against my eyes.

It's not that I don't think of you now,
while tending my spring tomatoes as you still shovel snow.

Months go by before I pick up the phone, and most days
it doesn't seem strange that you never do—

until I see my daughters,
asleep and holding hands, their legs entwined.

A ROOM THAT REMEMBERS LAUGHTER IS NOT EMPTY

I curl to sleep and smell from under my nails
onions I'd been chopping. It's true Frances,

lemon and vinegar would help, and I don't know
how to pray. Even without a body, you're both

cataract and sight. Do you blame me
the scuffed floor, the unpolished shoe?

My unruly garden shelters skunk. Fire-ant
mounds dot my lawn. Feral cats mark my house.

Cleanliness is next to godlessness, or never mind
lipstick left on my glass. I used to wear a gold ring

fat with pearls, but didn't know dishwater
would make it lose its luster. I soaped stains

with Fels-Naptha, and still did not add
a single hour to my life. It's okay with me

to grow afternoon drowsy with wine, eased
by trampoline springs squeaking under the weight of girls.

RECONSTRUCTION

Sister, you hold
a cup of tea against your chest, but

can't feel the heat. I ask
if your skin is smooth or scarred; you say

they saved your nipples. *Here,*
I'll show you, you say

as you move to lift your shirt.
I raise my hand, say *no*

before I understand what I've missed.

NORTHER

The wind triggers the motion-
                        detector lights.

A storm's coming. Finally,

a good change in the weather to clear
the bullshit of the day—
                        minor annoyances

that would amount to nothing if my parents
were newly dead.

But they're not. I hang on
to my father's loathing of gladiolas.

To my mother's mildew-pocked petticoats,
elastic waistbands so old

they crumble if touched.
                        Today,

so many small things went wrong,

but no one I know or love left me. And those
who have before, live in the night's wind.

Lessons

After a while you learn catsup
is not spaghetti sauce. Love
can be a grilled cheese sandwich
paired with tomato soup. You play Scrabble,
and learn you like to win. You learn war
can make a man see your favorite scarf
around your neck, and he must warn you
about surprise and strangulation. No BS
is the way to go, and it might not be all bad
to be alone. Dark days there's nothing
to learn. You scratch your scalp, fingernails
remind you at least you've grown past
digging half-moons into your palms.
Cottonwood tufts gather on a screen.
Traffic can sound like rain. Sometimes
people leave and don't come back, and
not everyone likes to watch a coming storm.

THE NEXT TUESDAY

Turns out, the roof's not fixed. Angel stuffed silk
and caulking to plug the drip, and now I sit

with a circle of rain. Well, well, who am I to think
I could keep it out? That's like saying heel-prints

across my brain are only memory, or Frances
in a clear bonnet could keep mist from her hair.

I can't control whether I say *fig* or if I fall
for the mechanic with a straight jaw. I can't say

rosary man who walks Broadway is made of flesh.
Or explain why avocado pits comfort

my mouth. It's cold and wet and what else
do I expect? Angel will come again with his tools.

He'll go back on the corrugated slope with the hose,
and I'll stay below to see what comes down.

GOING HOME

In my mother's house
        are many mansions. In her house
two hundred Sunday dresses
        hang by their necks. Sheet music
swallows the room where Elvis first appeared
        on Ed Sullivan, where sixty-seven Christmas trees
shone in the window, and ten clocks mark
                eleven different hours. In her house

I am a lost child. I rethink Dickinson
        to the tune of Amazing Grace. Rethink Jenny and me
in the dim garage lifting our shirts, the nearby church
        bells striking us out
                into sunlight without a word.

Her house is a hand-cranked music box
        looping Lennon's *Imagine.* Or, that's the sound
in my teeth. This house is
        my mother's adjustable skate. The missing key. It's

a sewing basket that has been passed down,
        and in it, a bright cushion stuck with pins.

What We Breathe

mold is just another word for stiff curtain

       not actually a curtain at all, but a throw rug rigged

on a tension rod to cover the basement window

       where thin light seeps in from the shadowy well

mold means mother

       I shook the curtain to see

              where you once let me keep kittens

sheltered in a wooden crate   long before

       I knew about sickness, except

              for the wheezy breath of the weakest

runt, a word

           sprung from the stump of an old, decayed tree

mold is not decay, it grows

       stubborn spores   rooted   in my body

       the place I left has not left me

           how long has it been making me sick?

my mother can't remember

a little more each day

who was at the front door   why is there a red truck?

can't remember

I'm in the house if I leave the room

FIRST FREEZE

When tomato vines go black, and my father spends the day
raking, slowly and in stages now,

my mother covers her geraniums with sheets.
I've traveled a long mile to buy this couple their milk.

I came to dress a wound on my mother's leg. To hear
the click of my father's rotator cuff. I can't

change the weight of coins in a coffee can,
the bathroom's pink tile, crackling grout.

In October's diminishing light, the sheet-covered mounds
glow, keeping those red clustered flowers ablaze.

As Always, Thirty Years Between Us

My father wants me to cut his hair
in the laundry room, where the rotary phone
still hangs on the wall. Here, I took
and made so many calls to boys
he disapproved of. This is an old story.
A father, daughter, half-regrets. I fold over
his ear the way he tells me to and trim.
Nothing's left of the lush, black swoop
or sideburns he always wore. I buzz
the white crown and snip stray hairs
from the bald part of his head. He's
not the man whose empty cans
I used to find in the trunk
of the car. I wonder, now, how
many times he knew my secrets,
but didn't say a word. No one
really can tell you how not to mess up
your life. When I was young,
I loved the winter nights, watching
my father grease fishing reels
at the kitchen table, cranking handles,
clicking spools shut. Summer was miles
away, but he took such pleasure
getting ready. Especially when it came
to sharpening his fillet knife. I leaned
my shoulder close to his, shut my eyes
to better hear him whisk
that blade across a wet, black stone.

RUSH OF PULSE AND SONG

Sometimes I hear a song and lean against the counter,
forehead in my hand. What happened
to afternoons tapped with rain and whiskey?

I have a room in my head, *Wild Horses* playing
as I taste my lover's kiss. Frances,

in the window, waves her arms, twisted with veins
that could circle our planet twice.
What good are capillaries if stretched 50,000 miles?

I understand pulse. I hear the rush in my ears.
Frances, on her back, pumps her legs in the air
to get blood moving. *Make hay while the sun shines,* she says.

What hay? What sun? I pour a drink and curl my tongue,
a soft funnel, so I won't burn my throat.

Frances climbs the ladder in my ear.
She's going to clean the gutters. Says
there's a lot of roof up there could use some sweeping.

AFTER MY FATHER'S FINAL
AND FAVORITE BROTHER DIED

Ray is gone, and in my father's voice,
a love I haven't felt since he bled in a quarter of his brain.

I sat beside him for days in the ICU, watching a documentary
where oceanographers fitted cameras with infrared lights.

My father, semi-conscious, lay hooked to machines.
It was a cold room, and in the deep
water, for the first time ever, the elusive
giant squid appeared in its natural habitat, alive.

I was ready for loss. Whatever my father didn't understand
about daughters, I let slip
through his calloused, unresponsive hands.
No one should have survived that bleeding, but he did.

Ray is gone. My father says
he filled with fluid. Ray's legs bloated
such that you wanted to stick a pin in and let them drain.
There was no way to release the water.

The nurses in the ICU made me leave my father's room
when I cried. "He needs to believe
he can come back," they said. "You're making him worse."

To attract giant squid, oceanographers
mimicked distress signals of jellyfish, because
squid prey on the creature causing the distress.

Like all cephalopods, my father has a large distinctive head.
So did his five brothers and when angry
their forehead veins popped out.

Only a week after his stroke, my father could speak again,
could make a fist and resist counter pressure.
We wanted shunts. He said no one
was going to take a saw to his head.

They'll bury Ray uphill from his brother.
"He can throw stones at Harold for eternity," my father says.
"Just like when they were boys."

Like a cephalopod, my father dives deep
into dark water on Tuesday mornings without Ray
at their table at Round the Clock. Without Ray,

my father dives to an incredible depth.
He is a giant of the ocean, hard to glimpse. He's

a tremendous swimmer, submerging
with the strength of eight arms
and the longest tentacles known to sorrow.

WHAT WILL BE LEFT

If you visit your mother, take off your shoes.
If she offers you tea, accept. When she says
she wants to lie down, try not to think about dying.
Go downstairs. Pass the washing machine,
your crayoned drawing of the White House.
Pass the exercise bike. Make your way through
suitcases, stacks of afghans, toys, boxes of spaghetti,
to the square dance dresses hanging from the pipes.
Take the yearbooks out of the rafters. Try not to think
about the cost of a dumpster. On good days,
she still sings. She doesn't feel bad about losing teeth.
Remember her silver fillings. Remember, standing together
at the mirror, your mother tonguing gaps in her open mouth.

MY MOTHER IN THE WINTER ZOO

Six peacocks sit like fat jewels shining in a bare tree.
It's Christmas and snowing so hard,

flakes pile high on telephone wires. We're nearly
the only ones here. You say you once came with your father

to see the oldest living cockatoo, before you knew
how soon he'd be gone. You never thought to ask him

who named you, or why at five you were dressed
in your Sunday best to join him on his bus route,

transporting German prisoners of war. You live
in a habitat of loss, where you scratch at the poor diet

of what you can recall, of what says:
these are the people I'm from. You refuse to leave

the lifetime of objects you've stored
down to a braid of your childhood hair. And here

we watch the pacing African wild dog whose paws
should never leave prints in snow, whose breath in this cold

ices his muzzle. The animal's worn path is a sorry replacement
for its instinct to roam. There are times I want to disown

my kind. But what's wild in me is tempered by the way
your hands involuntarily shake. You say, *Let's make*

our way to the wolves. We look through the one-way glass,
where within reach of us, the animal tears at a bone.

WINTER HAIBUN

Wind chill 51 below, the kind of day no one goes anywhere, only emergency workers. Nose hairs, eyelids freezing. Cars abandoned to the kind of snow everyone alive in '67 remembers, except mother's cousin whose death her daughter announces on FaceBook. Mother's sister-cousin, one of the last. My mother outlasts her own predicted decline and the freezing blast that cancels even delivery of the mail.

snapped power lines, frost-quake booms
my mother plays the piano

Half an Hour Before I Leave to Catch My Flight

The king no doubt is coming
                  for my mother, she for whom

clocks and calendars mean little
                  for whom

breakfast and birthdays blur, but
                  the piano unlocks

the chords, the words
                  I haven't heard for years.

The king is coming. The trumpet
                  yes, is sounding. Glory

glory halleluiah, my mother
                  is still my mother   then

she removes her glasses
                  and clicks off the light.

CHRONIC

There's no more waiting. The girls
      are grown. Soon

I will be alone. This is not

some new trick. So old, the lake
      knows what happens next. Waves

of undoing. Might quite be. My most vulnerable

daughter, after more than a decade of disease, unsheathed

      the needle, inserted—

finally,
and for the first time—

          her own infusion set

meaning: she now can save her own life.

Soon
there will be no need. No, need

      never ends.
          What is left to do?

Harbor

We don't give our children rocks to stay afloat.
Which isn't to say we haven't

turned stones to bread. But you should know

the ocean before you climb into the yellow raft,
where the jagged cliffs turn

into animals bearing teeth.
Your sad manicured claws are useless, and
you never taught your child to swim,

because years and years of entering the water
only to the waist have made your webbed feet

a joke. You are not the least of mothers
in the animal kingdom. You do your best,

guiding a tender-palmed hand
to plant star flowers. You gave your child a bed
of nectar-rich blooms to attract

winged-creatures that won't bite.

I WILL GROW OLD IN MY BED

—*after Cesar Vallejo*

On a calm night, when no one is looking,
I will grow old in my bed.
I'll be woven into the sheets. Don't look

for my body among the pillows,
on a Tuesday. Tuesday, because
everyone will have forgotten

weekend promises and about sleep.
One daughter will say goodnight
to another daughter, her voice carrying

the future down the hall. When they hear
"Mother," one will say, "She came to me
in a dream. I heard a peacock, but saw

a small pillow sewn full of beans."
The other will say, "I remember lavender,
and feathers across my eyes."

QUERY

If I said, *The peacocks in the gazebo*
woke me from a dream where someone shouted for help,
the sky yellowed, red lights flashed across a girl's face—

Would it be then that I was dreaming?
Frances, did you hear the peacocks?
Call for help? Where do those birds go?

Transformation of a Minor Goddess

My mother outruns the wind through spring roses,
    outruns the buzzers, the Price is Right bonus spin,

              faster than the god
who took her mother and left in her place

    a brick ranch house
            edged with perennials.

She outruns the wind of poor comfort

    to return to the meadow
        under this world, the meadow beneath

the worn carpet path
        beneath her window in the den

where she was   is now   called   was called

    child of the postmistress, flower

            of lost messages

daughter of burlap   of a sack full of seeds   unsown.

CENTO FOR THE SAME OLD

Forgive my tiresome nostalgia. Forget it.

Savage
and magisterial—

like a thirst for salt, for my childhood river
over which scavenger angels

pounce, claws
outstretched for the stumbling

me. And
now she
is gone. She

is one of many, so I drink to her and her and her—

AGAINST NOSTALGIA

I'm not convinced
that standing in the cemetery
long enough for the slow
dark to draw lightning bugs,

their fluorescence pulsing
over my parents showing me
their newly erected headstone
and where they'd like me
to plant hostas and geraniums
in the earth that will cover them

will do anything to relieve
the coming grief.   They're ready.
Forever
                    I've turned
my eye to the future,
blinked toward the new.

Once I thought
tragedy would define me,
something stray, a fast-moving
object lodged into my brain.

What defines me is constancy
of place, and my urge against it.

I've been going about this
the wrong way, licking
the same sore, gnawing,
trying to bite away the fleas.

PROPERTIES OF CHANGE

First there was the chicken coop.

Now wind whips fire
sparks embers from leaves.
Frances holds her hands to the heat, or

her paws. Or claws. Or fins if we were to trace
the origin of such strange tools. Frances

waves ash from my hair.
I don't want the smoke
to disappear. I've grown lone. Sinking

is one word for what happens to old foundations.

The coop was torn down. Its weathered boards stripped,
despite my tired wish
for the place to stay the same. Ashes

spiral from the burning can. Away from spirits

with nowhere to roost. Away from me,
swooning in leaf-smoke, hands coming loose.

The Above World

Today, a car spun across four lanes of traffic.

I'm blinking. I'm breathing.
Who's responsible

for that? This morning my girl cried for the tiger-tail guppy

languishing in her tank.
Is there any way to explain

what will follow the opening and closing of those small jaws?

That when gills stop,
      and the fish's companions descend to nibble its skin,

more than a body might be lifted
      beyond the filtered surface

          when a net swoops in and scoops it up?

PARTING THE DOME OF DARK SKIES

Mother, forget the way things look now—
for we both know

that when whatever it is
lifts the veil
there will be no astro-turfed yard, no neighbors

not the split-trunk
of your father's maple
grown through chain-link.

I've seen it too:
the black curtain, corners blown up.

Wind teases the edge,
but the planter at the corner of your lot
holds it down.

Let's not let the world fool us
with its presence.

Let's go into that absence

like the most remote part of West Texas,
where we might sit

under the star-pocked
dome of darkness, far from

cities and loves and sources
of light, molecules

bouncing in our ears,
in a silence that hurts to hear.

NOTES:

The poem "One of Those Days" owes its structure, flow of ideas, and very existence to Barbara Ras and her poem "You Can't Have It All" from the award-winning book, *Bite Every Sorrow*. I remain grateful for her model and influence.

The poem "Fourth Grade Autobiography" could not exist without the model and influence of Donika Kelly's poem that bears the same name from her award-winning book, *Bestiary*. Thank you, poet, for your example.

"Cento for the Same Old" is a cento borrowing lines from these poets and poems: Vievee Francis "Anti-Pastoral;" Alan Shapiro "Joy;" Stanley Kunitz "The Layers;" Elieen Myles "Transmission"

Laura Van Prooyen is author of two earlier collections of poems, *Our House Was on Fire* and *Inkblot and Altar.* She is also co-author with Gretchen Bernabei of *Text Structures from Poetry,* a book of writing lessons for educators. A graduate of the Warren Wilson MFA Program for Writers, Van Prooyen serves as Managing Editor of *The Cortland Review* and lives in San Antonio, TX.

CPSIA information can be obtained
at www.ICGtesting.com
Printed in the USA
BVHW030454250221
601055BV00003B/257

9 781734 786965